KUNDALINI

The Art of Kundalini Awakening

NICHOLAS WHITE

TABLE OF CONTENTS

INTRODUCTION

As a spiritual seeker, you attracted this concept of Kundalini awakening into your life as part of your own spiritual journey. This book is meant to serve as an all-inclusive guide to the knowledge of a Kundalini awakening so that you will have the capability to awaken it, and recognize its presence in your life. It is my hope that by the end of this book, you will depart with knowledge of Kundalini's historical context, a thorough understanding of what it means, why it is important, how it is awakened, and a strong comprehension of the results, advantages and even the potential side effects of this type of awakening. This book will also examine some of the scientific facts that support Kundalini's existence, and its potential to assist you, in your journey through life after experiencing this awakening for yourself.

This book presents not only the great advantages to such an awakening, but it also describes the potential dangers, as to provide a fair and balanced approach. It features the facts found throughout history, an explanation of what the experience is like, and a comprehensive approach in regards to how you can channel and retain the awakened state within you. I hope to provide you with a clear understanding of how and why this experience might be relevant to you. I will also address some of the issues that have been seen over the course of thousands of years, ever since this energy was first mentioned in religious texts. I will also provide tips and suggestions for how to prevent a potentially harmful spiritual awakening, which might occur if you are not prepared for this powerful experience.

I invite you to take this journey to spiritual awakening and learn more about the "coiled serpent" that lies within each of us, known as Kundalini. I provide you, the spiritual seeker, with facts and suggestions on how to properly guide yourself through an awakening experience—however, it is always helpful to seek out a spiritual guide in person. The best teacher or guide is a person who already went through the awakening process and who is an example of the type of spiritual being you admire.

The goal of this informative book is for you to take a journey through the historical path of Kundalini which might inspire you to ignite your own awakening right here and now. Throughout this journey, you will have explanations of the origins, history, religious ties and foundations of the sacred energy known as Kundalini. There will be an explanation about the advantages and benefits of a Kundalini awakening, as well as the potential unwanted side effects which can possibly occur without sufficient preparation. I hope you find this to be an informative guide and you walk away with a much greater understanding of this great energy. I invite you to join in this literary journey to find out how you can awaken a new spiritual power from within yourself.

Chapter 1

KUNDALINI HISTORY AND ORIGIN

As with any longstanding religious experience or practice, Kundalini hails from roots that are thousands of years old; specifically, the first mention of the Kundalini concept can be traced back to 9th century BCE. Kundalini was first mentioned in the Upanishads text that explores concepts of Hinduism's central philosophy. Interestingly enough, some of these common philosophies are seen in Jainism, Buddhism and Sikhism religions—I will touch on the different religious ties in the next chapter. The core of the Kundalini concept really refers to a spiritual and yogic awakening first coined by ancient Indian philosophy.

Historically, the next mention of Kundalini can be found in an 8th century work titled Ratnasambhava. In this Tantra text, Kundalini was referred to as a bracelet or ring, similar to a coiled rope. The next instance is found in the

12th century chronical of Rajatarangini. With Kundalini itself being translated roughly in Sanskrit as "circular or annular", it can also been seen used to reference "snake"— more specifically, as a snake-like energy that resides both coiled and dormant in the base of the spinal chord. We find that over the years, through these historical references, people are able to apply more appropriate terms for the energy that enables the spiritual seeker to envision and place more adjectives to the same type of energy all are seeking to explain.

Historically, the term Kundalini is next found in the Sarada Tilaka text which dates around the 11th century. Early on in the 15th century, Kundalini next appears as a technical term used by Hatha Yoga and then appears in Yoga Upanishads around the 16th century. Finally, in more recent history, around 1919, Sir John Woodroffe published a translation of the 16th century laya yoga treatises. Sir Woodroffe refers to Kundalini as serpent power, which is the common theme we see throughout the historical references discussed previously in this chapter.

In terms of the last hundred years or so, the Western civilizations have started to embrace Eastern philosophy, owing much of its rise in popularity to Carl Jung. In 1932, Carl Jung presented Kundalini to a psychological club in Zurich. In this presentation, he described a model for higher consciousness in individualization. Jung presented an idea to his colleagues that started the trend of embracing Eastern spiritual practices such as Kundalini yoga.

Also, in the 1930s, a duo of Italian scholars, Julius Evola and Tommaso Palamidessi wrote several books on

their interpretation of yoga in the form of alchemy (one can think of this as a type of magic). In their works they refer to Kundalini as "Serpentine fire" or "Igneous Power", and they compared them to the mystical science of Alchemy. Alchemy can be thought of as the combination of different essences or powers, which merge to create a magical reaction or tincture-like substance. Since its introduction to the Western spiritual world and culture, there has been a litany of other religious leaders who both utilized and spoke of the Kundalini awakening.

Most recently, at least since the counterculture and New Age movements gained traction in western civilizations, there has been a large shift in religious and spiritual awareness. Practices such as yoga and meditation are becoming more popular in modern society. These practices have proven helpful to millions of people who adopt an "Eastern" approach to both health and spirituality. Regardless of the personal reasons for adopting these practices, the impact has led to a mass exploration of spiritual enlightenment. Naturally, through the process of researching and gaining knowledge of these practices, people are instinctively seeking enlightenment, which leads them down the path of exploring a Kundalini awakening—just as you are doing by reading this book.

Chapter 2

RELIGIOUS REFERENCES
AND INTERPRETATIONS

As was discussed in the previous chapter, there are quite a few religions that made references to Kundalini in their scripture(s). Kundalini is not a religion in and of itself, but it is a spiritual process that is achieved through an increase in spiritual awakening or enlightenment. This awakening is said to sometimes come to people in times of turmoil and struggle, even if they are on a path of spiritual awakening. The awakening is a trend throughout India's many scriptural interpretations, some New Age beliefs and it's also seen throughout today's Western culture within different mindfulness and yoga based practices.

In Indian religions, there are a variety of Kundalini interpretations made throughout history and found in different religious texts. Essentially, the Kundalini awakening force is described in most of these Hindu-based texts as a dormant presence, or force within the human body. Furthermore, it is intimately connected with the chakra energy system (centers of psychic energy), nadis (channels of energy), prana (subtle energy) and bindu (essence drops). These energy references describe how energy is channeled throughout the physical body and ethereal human aura.

The energy is usually visualized and described as coiled, snake-like energy which lays dormant in the sacrum bone at the end of the spine. Throughout various texts, this Kundalini energy is said to reside anywhere from the navel to the spine, and it's most commonly found in the same snake-like form. This energy, if awakened, can cause a powerful and life changing experience. Before Kundalini can be awakened, a powerful period of enlightenment, self-actualization, and spiritual elevation should first be practiced in order to induce a positive awakening.

There are many historical references to Kundalini throughout different countries and civilizations. The Kundalini awakening is also referenced throughout European, Scandinavian, Middle Eastern, and even Latin American countries. Researchers found ancient artifacts and monuments that represent the power of the serpent. It's theorized that these societies understood the limitless nature of the human spirit.

References to spiritual awakening can also be found in Christianity, hence "the stairway to heaven." The cross is an excellent representation of Kundalini, which is demonstrated during the symbolic formation of the cross. The sign of the cross is actually symbolized by touching three different chakras and then connecting the pathway between them. The center ajna chakra, the anahata chakra, and the vishuddhi chakra are all involved in the symbolic representation (head, heart and moving across from shoulder to shoulder). There are many passages that speak to the power of the spirit, within the Christian tradition. There are also many biblical references to intense and overwhelming religious experiences that could be considered an awakening force, or a power so profound that the experience is life-changing and often leads to religious devotion. In the last century, there have been many religious figures and leaders who placed emphasis on spiritual awakening. This list includes Bhagwan Shree Rajneesh (also known as Osho), Aleister Crowley, and Gopi Krishna, amongst many other gurus in modern society. They all embrace both the yoga practices and Eastern philosophical teachings in general. In the New Age movement, there are many different sects that adopt the principles in their teachings and practices.

The common theme found throughout all of these different religions is that they seek to attain and share an intense spiritual experience for those who follow them. Although each religion uses different terminology to describe the energy awakened within a person, they all seem to share a similar terminology when describing the force. In a sense, it brings a certain amount of fluidity to these different branches of religious philosophy and joins them together with a shared aspiration to this sort of experience.

Another interesting fact about all of these different religions and cultures is that they all describe the potentially negative side effects that can be experienced during awakening. Each culture makes reference to negative side effects of people who have dabbled in a process that is over the heads or spiritual level, and they are then left in a state of seemingly disrepair. It is important to note that, despite the majority of interpretations that the Kundalini awakening is positive, there have always been warnings for those who may come up against something they are not ready for. As with unleashing any type of great power, Kundalini awakening should also be respected, and not taken lightly.

Chapter 3

THE MEANING OF
KUNDALINI

This snake-like energy is considered to be, interestingly enough, a feminine energy that is a huge potential source of psychic energy for one to tap into. It is believed to be coiled in or around the sacrum in three and a half circles, tail inside of its mouth, waiting to be awakened by a massive spiritual charge. Another fascinating trait of the Kundalini is that it is considered to be a source of creative energy that travels up and down the spine while igniting creative inspiration, psychic energy, and spiritual energy.

Throughout the texts, greater dissection of the actual model of the Kundalini serpent itself is explored. Within the lore of the Kundalini, it is said that the three coils the serpent is bound to represent the three mantras of Om—also known as past, present and future. They also refer to the three states of consciousness, which are sleeping, dreaming, and awake. Finally, the remaining half coil is said to be the transcendence being represented. Essentially, the meaning behind the three and a half coils exemplifies the entirety of the universe and the experience of transcendence and enlightenment.

It is interesting that the three seem to be representtative of the three fold path all share within Eastern religion. It is important to note the past, present, and future aspect of the three oms represented by the snake. In order to have a positive outlook on life, most of us look towards teachings of mindfulness that are represented by this mantra so we can fulfill a healthy living experience. Working towards greater paths towards awakening a new spiritual energy within ourselves, these are good words to help us categorize and meditate on to find a greater meaning.

The three states of consciousness, sleeping, dreaming and awake, are important aspects of life. Allowing oneself to explore through meditative practices these states of awareness, one can come to a greater understanding of what these mean for themselves. As most of us use these practices that involve basic yoga principles such as mantras, physical positions or postures within yoga or pranayama (which is breathing work done through the yoga practice), we build strength more readily within ourselves. The energy we create is said to move up the sushumna, in Western culture this could be seen as the central nervous system; in terms of the awakening, it could be referred to as the central energy channel.

Through this awakening, one is said to find purpose or enlightenment within their spiritual practice and life. The longstanding definition of kundalini states that one will

achieve Samadhi (or enlightenment) through the types of spiritual practices mentioned above. Once this level of enlightenment is achieved, it is said that they can stay in the state for long periods and consciously move in and out of it, directing the kundalini energy as the enlightened self deems appropriate.

Like all things good, kundalini awakening might also come with undesired side effects. During the awakening, this could include physical sensations such as itching, tremors or involuntary spasms, particularly in legs or arms, feelings of electricity running through the body or intense energy surges, there also may be uncomfortable feelings of intense cold or hot—usually this occurs as energy passes through chakras. People have also reported at times that they hear sounds or visions as energy passes through a certain chakra. One may also experience extreme sexual desires or even diminished desires as well. Others have reported issues with headaches or migraines, and even emotional upheavals, including symptoms from depression to antisocial tendencies and intense mood swings. Even more slightly alarming, some report disrupted sleep, pain in different areas of the body, and even a complete loss of appetite.

Some scholars of Indian philosophy also give credence to Kundalini as a near-death experience. Although not all who are awakened experience the same type of awakening, Gopi Krishna did state he felt that as he approached awakening, he was slipping into or was enveloped into a "Halo of light". Later in his life (after some reflection) he went so far as to refer to the awakening as a near death experience, due to the intensity and bright lights that seemed to envelop and surround him.

Kundalini awakening is a significant milestone on the path towards spiritual enlightenment. Different tantric texts describe Kundalini as the most primal of all energy, and yielding great power. We would possibly refer to this same type of energy as an unconscious power within oneself.

Chapter 4

KUNDALINI AWAKENING
BENEFITS AND POWER

There are many practices in Western society that have roots in Eastern cultural philosophy which promote states of relaxation, meditation and spiritual enlightenment. Most say it is best for an individual to have the guidance of a spiritual teacher to aid them in this powerful experience. An awakening experience is regarded by many to be something that is overwhelmingly powerful at times. As with tackling any new task, one should thoroughly research, prepare and ask for guidance, especially when it comes to approaching the task of kundalini awakening.

Initially, most people feel immediate benefits when this spiritual energy is activated. Cultivating this spiritual energy is something that will immediately lead to an increased sense of presence and awareness throughout daily life. Other benefits also include a heightened sense of body awareness, as well as increased energy levels.

Many also see the Kundalini awakening as a redirecting of creative energy within oneself. The practice is seen by the founder of Iyengar yoga, B.K.S. Iyengar, as a harnessing of creative energy, which can even be considered as the sublimation of sexual energy. According to Iyengar, this is said to occur from specific breath work and postures, and is not something experienced by those who only practice yoga a few times a week. As with most yoga masters, or those who practice yoga daily, repetitive practice and learning to stay in a desired meditative state is a skill that must be learned, practiced, and mastered. Through practice, however, Iyengar believed that this sexual and creative energy awakening could lead to a spiritual enlightenment.

There are also many reported health benefits that all stem from this awakening. Many who have experienced such an awakening claim they have increased physical strength, thought clarity, as well as improved memory capacity. Others also cite that there are physical changes that occur within them, including relief from liver disease, kidney stones, and even throat and stomach ailments. The balancing of the body through this awakening truly can bring one in line with the universe and their path to enlightenment. People report a multitude of physical ailments being relieved or even eliminated by the practices of yoga and meditation, including chronic ailments such as: high blood pressure, anxiety, and physical pain. In addition to the potential health benefits such as stress relief, mental stability, physical endurance and mental clarity there are additional qualities being researched by scientists today. Researchers have found evidence to believe that there are correlations between healthier bodily functioning, as well as strengthening one's heart and even improvement in areas such as lowering blood pressure.

The most important aspect of this process is that it introduces a new level of clarity, perspective, and understanding into your life. Awakening is a truly personal journey that is defined by a person's inner ability to tackle and achieve the highest levels of their conscious and subconscious mind. Through this practice, one gains not only the diligence, work ethic and spiritual happiness; they also gain the knowledge that they can put their mind to a goal and achieve it with enough hard work and effort. Awakening this energy is a simple reinforcement to the fact that you are a spiritual being who possesses infinite powers, well beyond what the naked eye can see.

The true importance of the awakening is that you should be able to live a happier and more spiritually connected life. It is important for us all to have balance within our lives, and we can truly start this process within ourselves by working towards a spiritual goal. The mental clarity that can be achieved through the perseverance and work that it takes to attain the awakening is something to be fully aware of as you move through the process. Being able to remain in control, yet open to new mental and physical experiences is important as you progress through new states of consciousness.

Many report this decrease in stress, and increase in enlightenment to be life-changing. It is important for a person to define what they wish to have happen in both their immediate daily life, as well as lifelong goals. By practicing and living a spiritual life, you can align yourself spiritually and energetically, in order to be the best version of yourself.

Chapter 5

HOW TO AWAKEN KUNDALINI

If you read until this point, then you should have a firm understanding of the meaning, history, origin, and benefits of a kundalini awakening. This chapter will explain the various techniques and methods about how it can be awakened.

The awakening itself occurs when the kundalini moves up the chakras of your spine, eventually meeting the Shiva (male energy), which yields the final result of enlightenment.

When Kundalini is both awakened and controlled in a positive state, then the practitioner is said to come in direct contact with Durga, or "mother of the universe."

When Kundalini is awakened, but uncontrollable, often resulting in a negative awakening fraught with many negative side effects, then the practitioner is said to come in direct contact with Kali, which conflicts with Durga.

These are terms to keep in mind as we move throughout the explanation and techniques of awakening. One shall always strive to call the goddess Durga into their awakening and prepare themselves to the fullest in order to avoid angering Kali by being ill prepared for the spiritual experience at hand.

These two goddesses represent the clash between light and dark, angels and demons, good and evil, infinite source energy and anti-source energy.

The various recognized spiritual paths to awakening kundalini include yoga, meditation, chakra energy work, and a series of techniques, exercises and strategies developed by those who have experienced a Kundalini awakening previously.

Each of these practices are sacred within both the physical and mental space in which they are practiced. A spiritual awakening should never be approached with anything other than reverence, respect, and an understanding for unleashing both great, but also unimaginable spiritual reactions.

There should be a creative approach to potential problem solving that one can develop by exercising their spiritual muscles, just as one exercises their physical body to prepare for a marathon or other similar physical journey. That being said, just as anyone would pack and prepare for a physical journey to another country or city, one must allow themselves to build a proper tool kit and prepare accordingly for their spiritual adventure. The tools discussed in this chapter are essential to assisting you in building your spiritual tool kit and exercising your spiritually enlightened muscles.

MEDITATION

One way to enhance your spiritual life and awaken Kundalini is to practice meditation. There are a multitude of ways to practice meditation, through chanting, or focusing attention on spiritual energy, to bring out and access your spiritual essence. As meditation is a practice where one trains their mind to come into an elevated state of consciousness, this is a large part of bringing the spiritual awakening into a person's awareness, and thus it becomes more likely to occur.

Meditation is a fairly broad term used most often to describe techniques that promote relaxation, and develop compassion, love, generosity and forgiveness while building one's life force, or energy. Meditation is meant to guide the practitioner into a higher state of well-being mentally, which should also reduce stress and promote a happier, more fulfilled life. It is expected that as a person rises in their level of spiritual focus through meditation, they will begin to be more in tune with their spiritual wants, needs and the ability to gain insight into both emotional and spiritual questions.

Meditation can be practiced by either sitting still or focusing the mind on a certain idea or thought. There are objects, such as prayer beads, designed to assist individuals with their meditation which are useful for training. The beads can be used as a reminder, to keep calm and meditate daily. Some people use meditation as a form of emotional regulation and control, which is part of the spiritual awakening process. Thought control is the first step towards being capable of controlling the energy between chakras.

As meditation is learning to control the mind, either actively or while sitting and practicing quietly, it will greatly assist any practitioner with their mental abilities in the long term and carry over into daily life while not being in a meditative state.

Meditation is often referred to as attaining a higher level of awareness through the practice of quieting the mind. This is in direct correlation to spiritual awakening and the goals that should be worked towards in order to reach that level of enlightenment. We can see the practice itself throughout thousands of years and it's also found in different religions, just as Kundalini is seen throughout these texts and cultures. From Eastern Asian religions like Hinduism or Buddhism, to Judaism, Islam and Christianity, the common principle of meditation is medicinal in nature.

Research has shown that not only does meditation affect performance in the workplace and learning, but it also increases social competence. Maintaining a quiet state of mind in any circumstance gives you the ability to be level headed and to think rationally in all types of scenarios. Since a spiritual awakening is an experience that leads to higher levels of consciousness, the ability to be ready (and calm) through the process is incredibly important.

YOGA

Hand in hand with meditation is the practice of yoga, which facilitates the channeling of peace by physical means through yoga poses and breath work. When it comes to bringing out the forces that allow for one to be spiritually awake within themselves, every type or branch of yoga can provide a person with an avenue for further spiritual awakening. By learning to take time and listen to your body as you move into different poses and positions, you are learning to push your physical, mental, and spiritual boundaries to new levels.

Yoga is a combination of mental, spiritual and physical exercises that stem from ancient India. Although there are many different Eastern religions that involve varying methodologies of yoga (ex. Tai-Chi), the well-known and most common types of today include Hatha and Raja yoga. There are a multitude of studies that found yoga to be an effective treatment for all types of ailments, ranging from heart disease to mental illness.

The etymology of yoga is essentially to join, unite or add together in a literal sense of any of these terms. Yoga is a physical practice combined with a meditative mental component and sealed with breath work. The special unison between both the body and the mind together is a potential gateway to spiritual connection with the higher self.

According to some, yoga ascribes to five basic principles, which represent the awakening that's experienced after activating spiritual energy. These five principles include controlling the body and mind, discipline, a connection with words such as mantra, a school or system of thought and philosophy, and finally the goal of the practice is to literally yoga—or unite.

Yoga is a practice that allows for an individual to fully develop skills they will need as they progress further down the path of spiritual awakening from within themselves.

Through the intense work using breath and movement in tandem, it will promote a sense of unity and harmony, which can be felt throughout the body.

Yoga is a powerful experience, and that becomes apparent as you advance through the practice, while tackling all of the physical and mental barriers along the way. Many of the poses in yoga trace back to thousands of years ago in origin, and the final goal is always the same.

All forms of yoga teach the student to be in tune with their body and mind. Those who practice it tend to have a greater understanding of the physical limits of their body, as well as a firmer grasp of their mental control and emotional stability. The human body is a complex biological "machine" that the soul inhabits. The mind and body are connected, and in yoga, controlled breathing is the glue that bonds the two together.

CHAKRAS

The energy chakras are crucial to the awakening process, since Kundalini itself is energy. The chakras are psychic energy hubs that are located throughout the body. They facilitate the flow of energy to and from. These chakras harbor the source energy that creates the very essence of "life" and consciousness within us. Chakras are said to be a part of what is called the subtle body, or non-physical parts of the body. These non-physical (subtle) parts of the body act as energy channels that are referred to as nadi. Nadi is what enables the body to be connected by a series of energy channels so that prana, or the non-physical life force vital energy, can freely flow between them. There are seven chakras that are considered to be the most fundamental to the physical body, although there are others that are reported in tantric texts.

The direct translation of the word chakra is seen most often as "circle" or "wheel". The chakra system is essentially a group of portal type hubs that are located around the central (spinal) part of the body, they exist in tandem with the breath channels, there are believed to be two side channels that cross at the central location of the chakras (allows for all the energy to be connected) and they are often associated with colors of deities. The seven chakras are said to be Sahasrara (crown chakra), Ajna (third-eye chakra), Vishuddha (throat chakra), Anahata (heart chakra), Manipura (solar plexus or navel chakra), Svadhishthana (sacral chakra within ones testes or ovaries) and finally Muladhara (root chakra located in the coccyx region).

The base energy chakra is Muladhara. This is often referred to as the root chakra as it is said to be the energy that roots you to the Earth, spiritually. Within this chakra itself there are three different qualities represented. They are called tamas, rajas and sattva. The sattva represents a harmonious balance, while tamas is considered a tendency to be lethargic, and in contrast, the rajas represents activity within the chakra. Once again, we see the three represented in the different trichotomy of energies in this chakra. Each person has their own personal mix of these three traits that root them to the Earth and the experiences they have, both consciously and subconsciously. Kundalini is considered to be residual energy that is stored in the region until it is awakened and moves up through the remaining chakras.

When energy moves up to the next chakra, Svadhishthana, or sacral chakra, it is said to represent our ability to be accepting of others, as well as new experiences. This second chakra is said to, when active and energized, help with the ability to not only accept change and feel creative—but it also is said to elevate the sexual energy of a person, which is why it is located roughly two inches below the navel.

Following this chakra is the Manipura or solar plexus chakra. This chakra is located at the navel. This navel chakra is said to be the source of our self-esteem, confidence, and will power. All of these are important traits in order to be secure with your personality, and your higher nature. This chakra is located in a person's core, which helps them to stand tall with strength and confidence.

The Anahata chakra is the next one, located in the heart area of the physical body. This chakra is key to the human experience as it holds one's ability to love. The chakra is located at the center of the chest, just above the heart and holds one's ability not only for love—but also for joy and inner peace.

Moving upwards we next come to the throat chakra, or Vishuddha. This is located, aptly named, in the throat. It is also said to be a place of energy used towards a person's ability to communicate. This chakra is important for any person, as it aids in self-expression for a person, their communication in general, as well as their ability to share their truth.

We next move to the third eye chakra, or Ajna. This chakra is one that assists us to see the bigger picture, as well as assists in one's ability to focus. This chakra plays a key role in the ability to meditate or practice yoga. It is the source of intuition and all other psychic abilities. It is located between the eyes on the forehead and it influences wisdom, decision making skills, and imagination.

Finally, the seventh chakra is the crown chakra or the Sahasrara, which is the final stop of the spiritual energy's path throughout the energy system of the human body. This chakra is located at the top of the skull, and therefore, it's the closest one to the heavens, it is aptly responsible for our spiritual connection to source energy and higher realms.

These seven chakras are the gateways for energy, and they are the same gateways in which the potent kundalini energy flows through. Intense focus and awareness of these chakras will enable you to control the energy flow within you.

It's crucial that all chakras are open and receptive in order for a Kundalini awakening to be triggered. A closed chakra could block the flow of kundalini energy and trigger undesirable results. A blocked chakra can be opened through intense focus during meditation, and also by resolving any conflicts in your personal life that might correlate to the type of energy of the specific chakra, as previously mentioned.

KUNDALINI AWAKENING EXERCISES AND TECHNIQUES

Although there are many methods out there, there is one easy, three step path to awakening a spiritual force within oneself. The spiritual path I recommend to anyone as a great place to start is to find a quiet place of meditation, focus on breath and finally verbally begin to express spiritual energy.

The first part of this process is to sit in a quiet place of meditation, and begin to focus energy and breathe into the base of your diaphragm as you inhale your breath. While inhaling, you should imagine and visualize the energy moving up from the base of the spine to the top of your head. This allows you to breathe through and move the energy upward. You should be relaxed and focused on your breath and moving the energy. With repetition of this, you should start to feel energy rising in a blissful manner. As you exhale, you should be concentrating on moving the breath from the crown chakra to the third eye and then the throat chakra, followed by the heart chakra. Then repeat the process over with each inhale and exhale. This is only one technique to trigger Kundalini awakening, there are many others.

There are also some techniques that focus on verbal chants rather than channeling energy through chakras via the mind. One common way that people channel energy in this way is through a meditative chant. This chant can be the name of a teacher that is enlightened and assisted you personally through your journey, or a Saint or Guru in your religion that has impacted you. As you repeat the name, you would inhale and again you would repeat the name as you exhale. This should bring their energy to you and assist you further in your Kundalini awakening. This is a commonly used spiritual technique that is thousands of years old—still used today as it is effective and powerful.

In addition to the techniques one can use, exercises have proven to be important connections to one's spiritual center. Physically engaging one's body in their spiritual quest has been very helpful for others in their awakening process. There are a few methods people have practiced in the past, one such method is Tantrism. Through this activity, the sexual chakra is freed from being trapped energy. As Kundalini and Shiva represent the male and female energies within everyone, this process of channeling one's sexual desires through vivid imagery and physical restraint is a potentially great source of assistance in awakening the Kundalini force. It is believed that one must be able to be in touch with both their masculine and feminine sides to create a balance within themselves.

Others turn to activities such as Pilates for physically exercising the body to channel and awaken the forces within themselves. Most cite that the big advantage of this method is to channel and physically engage their core based muscles and energies. There are many poses that engage the core, which is where the awakening occurs when energy is raised upwards from the spine to the head. The movements in Pilates can assist you with strengthening these energy flows. A large part of the Pilates practice is to channel and control breathing, which is also a large part of the meditative nature of a spiritual process or awakening. Other paralleled practices that are aligned with the awakening process are those of concentration, which is a necessity for Pilates practitioners, controlling their bodies (this is similar to the concepts of practicing yoga) as well as centering themselves in a physical manner. Finally, Pilates has a flow that is meditative, along with aligning one's posture through the process and finally allowing oneself to find relaxation in the whole process.

One final, and sometimes overlooked, tool for awakening Kundalini is through the use of music. Particularly, music that is repetitive and meditative in nature. Certain beats and tones can alter brainwaves and induce a meditative or trance-like state. It is recommended to sit in a quiet, dark place and turn the volume up loud enough that it drowns out any external noise, but also loud enough to hear all the parts of the music. It is another form of meditative energy where you quiet your mind and simply focus on the music. Music has been a creative and spiritual outlet for people across time, giving it the benefit of being seen as a source of these powers throughout time and cultures.

By utilizing all the tools within one's personal spiritual toolbox, one can only work closer to emulate and, eventually, achieve the Kundalini awakening within their spiritual mind. By allowing yourself to explore different methods that assist with spiritual practices, you open yourself up to a deeper experience.

Chapter 6

TIPS AND SUGGESTIONS

As with any new practice or experience in one's life, there may be a period of adjustment in understanding either how to achieve the goal or why it cannot be achieved easily. With a spiritual awakening, there is no shortage of potential struggles or trials that you may be put through by your own mind. Through this entire process, you should recognize that a large part of the process of awakening is in line with your ability to channel your own spiritual energies. As struggling is a part of any spiritual growth, I have found it always helpful to hear tips and suggestions from those that have already attained and achieved this awakening, which I hope to do for you in this chapter.

One important part of life is to know how to overcome struggles that may find their way onto your path. We all will struggle with certain aspects of working towards the spiritual awakening within ourselves and it is important to remember that what comes with struggle is an eventual ability to overcome. In fact, you should not feel as if you are struggling. A Kundalini awakening is something that shouldn't be forced, but rather invited to occur naturally when you are ready. This process is not something regarded as easy, as an awakening of this level should not come simply to those who ask for it. Many Eastern religions speak to the power and essence of life to be a struggle, as the greatest reward comes after the toughest of times.

Prayer can be an important component in spiritual awakening. Although one should pray to increase their relationship, one should never pray directly for something, even a spiritual awakening, as this may lead towards more material thoughts than the importance of the relationship. Others recommend that you should chant in prayer during physical activities like dance, walking or other aerobic exercises. Being able to channel energetic creativity through a spiritual chant can increase your spiritual connection. The meditative and repetitive motions of these activities can be great assistance, and as with any prayer or chant, it is desirable that they become second nature to you. One should look into the different mantras that may assist them and physical postures that have shown to be helpful during the process. Others also find the practices of both mindfulness and learning to achieve mental silence will assist them on their journey to quiet their mind and lead to awakening the Kundalini within themselves.

When it comes to awakening spiritual energy inside you, it is recommended that you find a spiritual guide to assist you through the process. Although not every spiritual guide has achieved a Kundalini type of spiritual awakening, most have worked hard to become a greater practitioner. A potential risk for one aiming to achieve this awakening is that they will overreach within their spiritual practice and try to progress too quickly. It is more difficult to awaken spiritual energy or energies earlier than you are ready for. This can potentially cause side effects that could harm both you and your spiritual progress and enlightenment.

There are some additional yoga-related tips to enhance spiritual prowess and achieve awakening. There are six basic yoga tips that can be used to facilitate the awakening.

- The first tip is to sit comfortably and practice deep breathing, while allowing the body to relax, gently loosening shoulders and neck muscles—even by slightly rolling or moving the joints themselves.

- Second, engage in a series of twists, while in a cross legged position. It is important to make sure you are both inhaling and exhaling as you twist. It is also important to constantly keep your spine erect and have good posture during the twists.

- Thirdly, you should do a powerful cobra pose. This helps to loosen the spine and, once again, remember to keep good breath throughout this pose.

- Fourth, you could practice the cat or cow pose, continuing to inhale and exhale and connect with both the breath, and the pose itself.

- Fifth, the most difficult of all the poses (and should be done only when ready and able to do so) you can take the flow of energy and reverse it by doing an inversion pose. This could be a shoulder or head stand—but should only be done when you are physically able to do so.

- Finally, lie flat, with hands to the side and feet open in a comfortable position. Then, close your eyes and release energy through gentle movements and breath. Remaining in this position for a good five to ten minutes is an excellent way to channel the energy that should grow and mature to attain the awakening of Kundalini.

These tips are good ways to physically condition the body and control breath, a very important part of any spiritual, meditative or yoga practice in general. You should never force yourself into a state that yields physical or mental strain. The best way in which to allow for enlightenment to occur is to pay attention to your body and mind, and know when to stop, after pushing yourself beyond your limits. People work many years to attain enlightenment and it is much better to reach awakening when you are ready, than to rush it. There can be serious negative consequences if one ignites a spiritual force such as Kundalini before being fully prepared for it.

UNDESIRABLE EFFECTS

In general, people have reported side effects most often when they rush to attain spiritual awakening before their mind and body is ready for it. When this occurs, the energy can be diverted into other channels in the body that can cause physical or emotional distress. Within the body, the energy that should flow through the central spinal pathway is instead channeled into intertwined energy paths known as ida, pingala or nadas that actually wrap around ones spiritual enlightening sushumna and allow for the negative physical and emotional interactions.

Some report that there are dangerous side effects to spiritual awakening that potentially stem from a person's non readiness for the intense awakening process. There are reports of individuals who are emotionally upset and traumatized by the intensive process that occurs when one awakens the serpent energy of Kundalini in particular. Some people report feelings of guilt, anxiety and confusion; at times they feel depressed as well. Sometimes these intensive emotions are intertwined with intensive feelings of wholeness and bliss. However, there are reports of the negative feelings taking over individuals who are unable to process and handle the awakening that has occurred within them. It is suggested for those that experience this negative side effect that they should practice exercises that are able to ground themselves in nature, a very healing force.

Others have stated that the premature burst of spiritual energy has actually led them to a psychotic breakdown. Although this is not widely reported, there are still some that experience the intensity to the point where they are unable to connect with physical reality and may seek psychiatric treatment. Although there is no firm scientific evidence to solidify the following; some people report that medical intervention may complicate the process. It is important to have a guide through the process, someone like a therapist or psychiatrist, involved to assess any potentially dangerous situation like this. This is a reason I believe that one must learn more about the awakening in order to deal with the changes within themselves. Although there is no scientific data to support these assertions, one should always prepare themselves for the worst possible outcome to the best of their abilities. If the negative consequence occurs from your spiritual practice, then seek help that allows for you to heal and understand what happened, so that you can begin the healing process.

Chapter 7

SENSATIONS OF KUNDALINI AWAKENING

Although no two people experience anything exactly the same, for a spiritual awakening, there are some clear descriptions in a few different texts that explain possible sensations. Being open minded and mentally prepared for something new is a great basic mindset to put yourself in.

You may experience temperature related sensations in the base of your spine. For some, this experience could feel intensely hot, and for others, pleasantly warm. As the energy is channeled upward, it begins to grow as it activates the other chakras along the way. Once the energy reaches the crown chakra, then the heat sensations may shift to a cool, or even a cold feeling as the energy is spread throughout the body.

Once the Kundalini energy reaches the crown chakra, then it's also possible to have physical, auditory, and visual experiences that can be intense, and even disturbing. There are reports that range from trembling, feelings of extreme temperature changes (from hot to cold) and also the feeling that the body is rocking and vibrating in an almost violent manner. Many report hearing potentially strange and somewhat unpleasant sounds that are accompanied by seeing lights. The lights seen can come from outward, unseen energy forces, or even from within themselves, as Gopi spoke about in an earlier mentioned quote.

These experiences and sensations could last from seconds to several minutes. During this time, the practitioner should attempt to raise the Kundalini energy to their crown chakra, meeting up with the Shiva (male counterpart) which causes enlightment. The intertwining of these two opposite counterparts of energy helps a person to reach their awakened state. Once the masculine and feminine energies are combined, then the next step should be to transfer the energy back down to the heart chakra. This is because the lower chakras tend to lead to a host of potential problem sources, such as ego inflation, which is not complementary to the awakening. It is said that the more one practices raising the Kundalini to the crown and down again, the more likely it is for the energy to remain where it is moved to most—aim for the crown and heart.

A Kundalini awakening, or any spiritual awakening, is defined by some as achieving a new level of consciousness. From meditation, to yoga and accessing and being familiar with chakras, then all of the work and effort taking place is to lay the foundation to open the mind to greater spiritual experiences.

With any spiritual process, there is unknown territory to be discovered, and as the energy and light moves through your body, you should be able to, even if it is at times uncomfortable, know that the experience is leading you to a new spiritual level of attainment. Most reports of people who have achieved the awakening are inclined to share their experience with others. One who is awakened is reported to feel more in tune with themselves and the world around them, adding to their desire to share more of themselves. This enables you to provide guidance so that others can also achieve the awakened state.

Those who have attained this awakening are those that have made enlightened practices like yoga and meditation a part of their lives for many months, if not years. One should not attempt to jump into the practices of yoga and meditation and immediately find themselves ready to awaken powerful spiritual energy. In fact, it is very advisable to take much time and effort in developing the basic skills such as meditation and yoga until you are comfortable and well-grounded in these practices. You will begin to thirst for a greater spiritual experience and while you listen to this, make sure to prepare yourself to the highest degree possible. You will know when you are ready. In one sense, a person ready for an awakening should feel they have worked towards the practice and gained a new understanding of life itself before they attempt the awakening process.

It is also greatly emphasized to have a higher understanding of chakras and how to harness the energy within them. With the help of this book you will have a generalized guide to understanding the 7 main chakras, but it would also be beneficial to research more about them on your own. Through your practices that work up to awakening spiritual energy, you should have greater awareness of your body and how to channel energy through your own chakras. Essentially, a large part of the awakening process is to fully develop, understand and know how to control your mind and body into a transitive, meditative state of peace. You also need to learn how each chakra feels as energy passes through it. This state you will reach will help you to feel more comfortable as the enlightened awakening of the Kundalini channels through you.

When you are ready for Kundalini awakening, then the experience itself should feel very natural and blissful. Ideally, an awakened person should be able to feel and control the Kundalini energy throughout their chakras. Knowledge of your own body and mind are important aspects that should be engrained into you before you begin to attempt to awaken any powerful spiritual energy, such as Kundalini. Although there can be many great advantages to awakening powerful spiritual energy, you must always keep in mind that, without proper guidance and work, there can potentially be hazardous results if you try to force the awakening process prematurely.

Chapter 8

POTENTIAL SIDE EFFECTS
OF KUNDALINI

lthough a spiritual Kundalini awakening is seen by most as a wonderful, powerful spiritual experience, there are those that see harsh side effects or claim there is no positive energy that comes from it. Within the psychological community, the Kundalini is actually classified as subconscious energy with the potential to be dangerous. Probably the most renowned medical professional to actively describe Kundalini was Psychiatrist Carl Jung, the founder of analytic psychology mentioned earlier. Through his work with the unconscious mind, Jung has actually been speculated to have had his own Kundalini spiritual awakening experience. Throughout his life, Jung spoke of and lectured about Kundalini and its potential to both enrich and bring harm. Jung understood the power that this energy could have over a person and he was determined to bring it to the attention of the Western world at large.

Jung was a Swiss born psychiatrist born in 1875 who was at the forefront of the analytical psychological movement of individuation. This type of psychology includes concepts about collective unconsciousness that Kundalini is considered to lie dormant within. We now know that Jung reported in 1913 that he had his own unconscious confrontation with, what he refers to as, "active imagination where he saw visions and heard voices". An important precursor to the Kundalini awakening is physical, mental, and spiritual preparedness or it can create a traumatic experience for the individual, which Jung confirmed was the case for himself. As Jung did a lot of work throughout his career on the unconscious mind and its power over a person's psyche, he seemed to always add his own personal mention of spiritual experience as a cause of harm.

Jung describes the awakening as a movement of the unconscious and conscious processes of the mind. The awakening was used by Jung to explain the ability to experience and describe elements that exist within each of our unconscious minds, if they are overwhelmed with an energy they are not ready for. Jung actually cautioned in his works that, for Westerners, yoga may dominate both the body and unconscious mind while ascending into the higher chakras, possibly creating spiritual traumas. Essentially, Jung saw the potential of this awakening to be so great, that it could transform lives beyond a rational level of comprehension and comfort. Jung's possible spiritual trauma is chronicled in a personal journal known as "The Red Book". This brings a documented and potentially public case for scholars of today to examine and learn about his experience.

In Hindu texts, as mentioned above, a premature awakening is referred to as summoning the Goddess Kali. Kali is said to be a source of terrible power that is released if Kundalini is awakened without the necessary preparation. She is also said to rise in anger and her ferocity can frighten all who come into contact with her. Kali is said to seek vengeance and can only be calmed through the power of prayer, which diminishes her presence. There are also reports, unlike most that state Kundalini is benevolent and beneficial, that pose the question of some historical figures suffering from this awakening. These claims are made about the historical figures of Saint Theresa, zen master Hakuin and Nietzsche—who all did great work for the world, but suffered internal struggles. There is also a researcher, Dr. Johnathan Shay, who did research regarding Post Traumatic Stress Disorder of individuals who had undesirable Kundalini symptoms that plagued them. In his work, he explores the power that could potentially manifest itself in the human brain as a type of trauma if one is not ready and prepared to receive the awakening, which he states, is the cause of PTSD symptoms.

Since the 1960s, Western society has seen a great influx of Eastern religious cultures and ideals in our society. Research into the effects of meditation and yoga is becoming more widespread. As fields such as near-death studies and transpersonal psychology gain more credibility, an underlying psychological imbalance is being noticed as westerners attempt to comprehend eastern religious practices.

It is thought by some professionals, that experiences with a powerful spiritual energy, such as Kundalini awakening, can go awry and actually be viewed by some as "psychotic episodes" (as briefly mentioned during the section on Carl Jung's experience). This is due to the fact that people who awaken Kundalini often don't have the proper fundamental mental and spiritual framework to safely control such powerful energy. There are even some reports that epileptic patients might in fact be experiencing extreme uncontrollable cases of Kundalini awakening. These reports consist of people stating feelings of pain across their lower back and moving all over their bodies. Sometimes people report a high pitched noise, similar to tinnitus, which would move through different levels of intensity. Some even claim that it feels as if their head is on fire. All of these symptoms are commonly found in cases of uncontrollable Kundalini awakening.

There is also a growing study that is termed by researchers as Kundalini syndrome. Instead of referring to a single event that incites potentially harmful side effects, researchers describe this as something that could occur over a period of months or even years. The patients in these cases are mentally destabilized in a state of spiritual upheaval and panic.

It's important to pay close attention to these symptoms as you progress through the awakening process yourself. There can be a litany of physical and emotional issues. Side effects can include anxiety, depression, psychological torment, frequent headaches and gastrointestinal issues. Sensations of heat, cold, and electricity-like energy radiating throughout the body are also reported. If these extreme symptoms are experienced, then it is advisable to seek help from a doctor to confirm that there are not any underlying medical issues causing the problems.

The proper groundwork of healthy spiritual principles and practices is the key to whether or not someone experiences a positive or negative spiritual awakening. Someone who is prepared for this experience is more capable of maintaining control of the energy throughout the chakra system in order to attain a higher level of spirituality. Whereas someone who rushes into the experience unprepared will be at risk of losing control and possibly causing spiritual trauma. To prepare and study spiritual practices is something that people work towards for the entire lives. It's important to take things slow and pay attention to your physical and mental state. If you have done the necessary work to lay a strong spiritual foundation, then you are well on your way to channeling a positive enlightening awakening.

Chapter 9

THE 7 SIGNS OF A
KUNDALINI AWAKENING

The Kundalini awakening experience is profound, enlightening, and blissful. You will know when it occurs because there is no mistaking it. It will elevate your consciousness and awareness to a level that you haven't previously experienced in your lifetime. It will likely alter your entire perception of life, death, and reality. Here are 7 signs of a Kundalini awakening that you might experience:

1. **Increased Intuition**

Intuition is that "gut-feeling" or instinct that you feel in response to a specific person or circumstance. In many ways this could be considered a sixth sense, or psychic ability. As you progress through your spiritual or Kundalini awakening, you will become more aware of these sensations, and they will be much more present. You will gain access to greater insights and be able to analyze a situation quickly based on instinctive feeling rather than conscious reasoning.

Intuition is a spiritual guidance system that is given to you by your higher self to keep you on the correct path.

An indirect effect from increased intuition could be elevated intelligence and IQ. This is because you will be able to analyze problems using both conscious reasoning and intuitive guidance. As a result, you might find yourself being able to make correct decisions faster, and learn new skills quicker.

2. Greater Ability to Understand Different Perspectives

All life and consciousness is connected to source energy, so even though people tend to view a specific situation from only their own perspective, it's possible to also have an understanding of others' perspectives of the same situation because of this universal connectivity. As Kundalini rises upwards through the chakra system of the body, it's going to bring you more in touch with source energy, thus the ability to understand other perspectives much easier.

Kundalini awakening will change the way you perceive individual situations and the world in general. You will start to see the world without any "filters." Although this is a very profound capability and experience, it can also be lonely, in a physical sense. The reason is because others who have not experienced a Kundalini awakening will still be grounded and limited to understanding only their own personal perspective. In other words, they simply won't be able to comprehend your understanding and perception of the same situation because you are on an entirely different level of awareness and reasoning. As a result, you might find it harder to relate to others.

3. Mood Swings

One of the side effects of a Kundalini awakening is a flood of mixed and confusing emotions. Since Kundalini flows through the very essence of your being, it brings you into higher states of awareness and enlightenment. This is very positive, however, this doesn't necessarily mean that all of your prior lower vibrational emotions, beliefs, and values simply vanish. The mixture between higher awareness and prior low vibration emotions can leave you in a state of contradictory confusion. This is what will cause a flurry of mood swings. In order to remove your prior emotional baggage, you need to bring it to the surface and confront it head on. You need to understand why you had your prior emotions, and accept them as part of the awakening experience. Only then can you begin to leave them behind you and truly move on to higher vibrational states of enlightenment.

4. Changes in Appetite and Diet

As you progress through a Kundalini awakening, you might notice a substantial decrease in appetite. The reason for this is because you are channeling much more prana through your chakra system than prior to your awakening. This increase of life force energy will keep you feeling much more energized, whereas before you might feel the need to eat a meal in order to obtain a similar, but different level of energy. After your awakening, you might find yourself gravitating towards sun light and fresh air in order to extract more prana, instead of seeking your next meal.

Along with your decreased appetite, you might find that when you are hungry, your food preferences change.

Your state of mind affects your energetic vibration, but your diet also plays a major role. Food, just like everything else, carries its own specific energy vibration. It's no coincidence that vegetarianism, veganism, and other similar diets are common among those who practice yoga, meditation, and other spiritual practices regularly. Fruits and vegetables are very high vibration foods because they are cultivated from the sun. Meat, dairy, and other animal food sources carry a much lower vibration. One reason is because animals in the meat industry are often subjected antibiotics, growth hormones, and other artificial substances. The other reason is related to the treatment of animals in the meat industry. The animals often live in terrible conditions. These conditions trigger emotions of fear and stress within the animal, and those emotions are transferred energetically to their meat. So when we ingest this meat, we are also ingesting those low negative vibrations that were experienced by the animal while in captivity. So as your energy rises, you will most likely start to gravitate towards fresh plant-based foods naturally.

A plant-based diet is beneficial for the mind, body, and spirit. These high vibration foods will keep your vibration high. It will also have a positive impact on the body itself, which is related to the PH level. Meat, dairy, sugar, and artificial preservatives or unnatural chemicals lead to a buildup of acidity within the body. There are many scientific studies that suggest an acidic body provides the necessary breeding ground for bacteria, disease, and other physical ailments to thrive. On the other hand, disease and bacteria simply cannot thrive within an alkaline body. Therefore, a plant based diet, which is very alkalizing, will improve bodily health drastically.

A good way to determine your body's PH level, and simultaneously start to alkalize it, is to squeeze the juice from a lemon into a glass of water and drink it daily. This might sound counter-intuitive due to the high citric acid content of lemons, and that is true. However, once the lemon is metabolized by the body, then it has a very alkalizing effect. The first few times you do this; the lemon water might taste extremely sour and be very unpleasant. If that is the case, then it is a sign that your body has an acidic PH level. As you continue drinking lemon water daily, you will begin alkalizing your body, and after a while the lemon water will lose its intense sourness, and start to taste like lemonade. One important point to keep in mind is that the lemon water is not yet metabolized by the body when it enters the mouth; therefore the citric acid content is extremely high. For this reason, it's strongly recommended to either eat food or brush your teeth afterward to remove the acid from your teeth; otherwise you risk erosion of the tooth enamel.

5. Heightened Sexual Experiences

Kundalini energy is stored in the second chakra, near the loins. As this energy is channeled upward through the other chakras, then it changes the way you feel sensations during sexual acts. For males specifically, a Kundalini awakening can cause different types of orgasms. The reason most males don't experience multiple orgasms is because they are often cut off from the second chakra, so that energy never travels upward. This is why they often experience one type of orgasm. For females, their chakras are naturally more open, and this why they are more prone to experience different types of orgasms with little or no energy work. So when males are able to open the remaining chakras, shift their awareness, and channel that energy upwards, then their sexual experiences become much more profound.

6. Increased Desire to Relocate or Travel

As your energy vibration increases through Kundalini awakening, it's common to get spontaneous desires to move around or travel. Energy fluctuates in different areas, and you may be drawn to places with higher vibration. For example, if you live in a big city, then you might find yourself wanting to spend more time in parks and in other places with nature, as opposed to the crowded inner city. Densely populated areas can harbor a lot of low vibrational, grounded energy. This is in contradiction to Kundalini awakening, which facilitates the flow of energy through you, as opposed to keeping you grounded.

Similarly, you might also have the desire to travel greater distances to new places. As your energy vibration raises, your awareness shifts, and your perspective changes, then you will often seek new experiences which promote further spiritual evolution.

7. New or Changing Interests

As your Kundalini rises, your energy vibration elevates and your creativity increases. You might seek new outlets for this new found sense of inspiration and creativity. You could find yourself turning to writing, art, music, and other similar activities that allow you to channel that creative energy in a positive way.

In more extreme cases, this could lead to a desire to change your entire lifestyle or even your career. You will instinctively seek work that you are more passionate about and derive fulfillment from. This is an important sign because your new desires will often guide you down a path that was right for you from the start.

Chapter 10

LIFE AFTER KUNDALINI
AWAKENING

Although every spiritual program will outline the advantages and results that are expected to be gained by practicing the recommended philosophies; a spiritual awakening is a unique experience as it is attained through hard work, personal growth, and expanded awareness. These are very personal concepts. A Kundalini awakening advances spiritual development, elevates the consciousness to new levels, and yields a happier fulfilling life. The positive results from the awakening include healing, peacefulness, enlightenment and a resounding new depth of spiritual understanding.

In terms of physical healing, there are clear advantages to both physical and emotional well-being post- awakening. The human body is composed of a mass of cells that are constantly creating energy and working together to promote health and healing. These cells are always multiplying and dying off in mutual harmony. In fact, every seven years, all the cells of your body are reborn. In this sense, you inhabit a brand new body every seven years. The flow of energy throughout the body ensures that these cells multiply correctly so that you can maintain excellent health.

The powerful aspect of the awakening and regeneration of energy within yourself creates a powerful healing that will elevate you to a new state of consciousness. Although spiritual awakening is perhaps not at first thought of a healing energy, it truly can create a cycle that allows you to start to heal past traumas you have dealt with. With a new, revitalized sense of understanding obtained by this new transitive, enlightened state, it will shift your focus so that you live in the present and embrace all that comes with daily life. Most of us become entrenched with the need and desire to continually relive the past, or focus on the future, when the majority of importance in life is in the present. By shifting your awareness to the present you will alleviate previous emotional burdens. This spiritual reformation and present mindfulness is the source of emotional healing.

Spiritual awakening can help you achieve a new sense of peacefulness in life. By allowing yourself to focus on being present in the moment, you can start to find inner peace. Although there are aspects of meditation and yoga that are frequently used as stress management techniques for many people, allowing yourself to have the intrinsic motivation to achieve a greater level of enlightenment adds more to your tool box of gaining and attaining inner peace. Through the fundamental practices you learned to use daily, you not only achieve personal peace, but you also pass that along to others who come in contact with your high energy vibration. You will be able to connect to others in a much deeper way. As you are a beacon of this new powerful energy, you may even bring new, revitalized romantic connections into your life.

As people feed off each other's energy without even realizing, achieving a sense of inner peace and tranquility will attract others to you intuitively. This ability to remain calm and peaceful can serve you well in many aspects of your life. Not only will it allow you to start and end your day with a peaceful mind set, but you will be able to take a calm and rational approach to any situation or problem that arises. Working towards this spiritual journey to awakening will help you be rooted very firmly in your spiritual practices.

Enlightenment is the ability to identify the complexities and intricacies of a situation, and have awareness of the different perspectives towards it. In terms of many traditional translations of the word, it means to be fully awakened and to have gained insight into the inner workings of the mind and spirit. It also represents, particularly in Hinduism, an end to suffering within the reincarnation process that we are all bound to.

Finally, you will have a much better understanding of spirituality and how to enrich your daily life. As we mentioned above, positive awakening experience of Kundalini is referred to as Durga. This stems from what is referred to as a refined symbol of the unconscious. Seated on a tiger within Hindu mythology, Durga is said to be a beautiful goddess with 8 hands, these representing man's eightfold elements. She also wears 52 prayer beads that are human heads to symbolize her power, as well as representing the 52 letters of the Sanskrit alphabet. Durga's powers are said to give peace and power to all, as well as to protect against all evil and temptation.

In order to achieve optimal results, it is not necessary to use her as a spiritual guidepost; however, it could certainly be beneficial to focus on her energy as you progress through the awakening.

CONCLUSION

I t is my hope that you have a greater understanding of Kundalini within historical, religious, and scientific contexts. A Kundalini awakening is the channeling of dormant, sacred spiritual energy upwards through the chakra system. The end result is an increase of self-awareness, creativity, inspiration, and spiritual enlightenment which brings about feelings of peace and bliss. Awakening Kundalini will give you a new found perception of life, death, and reality.

It is crucial to approach this awakening in a slow and methodical manner, for your own physical safety, and mental sanity. Practice meditation and yoga regularly, and familiarize yourself with your chakra system. Learn to control the energy that you are channeling through you. If necessary, seek additional guidance from a trusted spiritual teacher. Do not rush this process. The majority of the satisfaction you will derive will come from the spiritual journey itself.

If you manage to awaken Kundalini, then pay close attention to the physical, mental, emotional, and spiritual changes that follow. In a sense, you will be reborn, so it's important to adapt to your new level of awareness. Embrace the sense of enlightenment on every level of your being because it is a glorious taste of who you really are. You are a spiritual being with unlimited power to create. Time and space, as you understand it in this physical life, does not exist because you are infinite in spirit. Kundalini awakening will bring you one step closer in touch with your higher self. I wish you a safe and peaceful spiritual journey.

www.ingramcontent.com/pod-product-compliance
Lightning Source LLC
Chambersburg PA
CBHW072113280526
45788CB00006B/2513